LIBRARY OF CONGRI

Lent with the sain

ISBN 978-1-61636-131-0 (alk. paper)
1. Lent—Prayers and devotions. 2. Christian saints. 3.
Catholic Church—Prayers and devotions. I. Title.
BX2170.L4F75 2012
242'.34—dc23

2011035255

ISBN 978-1-61636-131-0

Published by St. Anthony Messenger Press
28 W. Liberty St.
Cincinnati, OH 45202

www.AmericanCatholic.org
www.SAMPBooks.org

Printed in the United States of America.
Printed on acid-free paper.

12 13 14 15 16   5 4 3 2 1

Contents

Third Week of Lent

Fourth Week of Lent

· · · | · · ·

Introduction

Each year as Lent begins, I look for an old keepsake—
My Lenten Missal, published by the Confraternity of the
Precious Blood when I was in grade school in the 1950s.
It contained the prayers of the Mass and the readings
for every day of Lent. Modern illustrations—many
showing the biblical characters in modern dress—
captured my imagination. I followed the Mass (still in
Latin) daily, which we attended as part of our Catholic
school routine.

This missal stressed the traditional keeping of Lent.
In those days Catholics had to keep a rigorous fast from
food. Grade-schoolers like me gave up candy or other
treats. We attended the Way of the Cross each Friday in
school and on Sunday afternoons. Attendance at the
Stations was mandatory on Sundays, even after you had
gone to Mass that morning.

Lent was a serious time of penance, with an emphasis
on personal conversion and turning away from sin. The
suffering and death of Jesus was the focus of the season.

When I was in the seventh and eighth grades I was an altar boy and served at the special liturgies of Holy Week. An innovative assistant pastor even taught us to chant some of the prayers for those days in Latin. I looked forward to going back to church on Holy Thursday evening to pray before the elaborately decorated altar where the Blessed Sacrament was reserved.

Throughout these years, I've kept that missal, partly from nostalgia. It reminds me of what Lent meant to me in the "first" part of my spiritual life—which actually continued through my seminary days.

Since my ordination as a priest, the meaning of Lent has changed. Now—especially in my current assignment as a pastor—my Lent is focused on making of new Christians. The Rite of Christian Initiation of Adults (RCIA), and the Second Vatican Council's "refocusing" of Lent around the preparation of candidates for baptism, has meant a different kind of personal "keeping" of Lent as well as a different focus in preaching and liturgy. For Catholics, it is a time to renew our baptismal commitment while praying with and for those entering the church at Easter.

Our lenten penitential practices remain an important part of Lent. Now, however, we choose them with an eye on renewing our identity in Christ, even as we continue to "turn away from sin and believe in the Good News," as one of the prayers for the distribution of ashes says.

In choosing the saints to accompany your prayer and reflection, I have kept this renewed purpose of Lent in mind. I was guided in my choices by themes of conversion and identity with Christ, using the daily readings for Lent as my inspiration. Occasionally, I picked saints who are more prominent or especially connected to our time. I've tried to keep some diversity in my choices as well.

To mark most of the lenten Sundays, I used important Old Testament figures along with St. Paul and St. Clare—the latter for a special reason. In the year of this book's publication, it will be eight hundred years since Clare left her family's home on Palm Sunday night to take on the habit of a nun and follow the gospel way. My sisters in our local Poor Clare community suggested Clare for Palm Sunday!

I would like to dedicate this little book to my Scripture professor, Fr. Hilarion Kistner, O.F.M. He taught me New Testament thirty-five years ago and preached at my first Mass. I have, in recent years, had the wonderful privilege of working with him at St. Anthony Messenger Press. Truth be told, I believe I am a more attentive student of his now than I was in the seminary.

Fr. Hilarion is always ready to answer my biblical questions and to look over my writing for any potential heresies. He adds nuances and insights from his years of scholarship and is willing to entertain my theories. He shares his latest insights from his prayer, reading, and study. And he does it all with wonderful humor and grace. It's a great gift to have a great teacher; it's an even greater gift to have him as a friend long after the class-room. Thanks, Fr. "Hank"!

· · · | · · ·

Ash Wednesday

Do You Want to Be a Saint?

JOEL 2:12–18; PSALM 51:3–4, 5–6, 12–13, 17;
2 CORINTHIANS 5:20—6:2; MATTHEW 6:1–6, 16–18

In *The Seven Storey Mountain*, the Trappist monk and spiritual writer Thomas Merton explains how, when asked by his friend Robert Lax what he, Merton, wanted to be, he replied that he wanted to be a good Catholic. Lax, a poet and mystic, told him, "What you should say is that you want to be a saint." Merton deferred, conscious of his own failings and inadequacies. But Lax persisted: "All that is necessary to be a saint is to want to be one." By desiring sainthood, Lax said, we consent to become what God has created us to be. God, in turn, will make us saints.[1]

As we begin these lenten meditations with the saints, it may be helpful to remember that the foundation of Lent is our baptismal identity with Christ. This season prepares those who seek Christ for baptism; those already baptized use this time to renew that identity.

In singling out exceptional followers of Christ, we don't want to forget that all Christians should desire to live forever in the eternal life of God. Such a goal is the fulfillment of our Christian identity. That's another way to describe sainthood. And it's also a good goal for our lenten prayer and practice.

Today's Action

Who is your favorite saint? Read the life of that saint, whether online or in a book about saints, and choose some of the saint's qualities that might influence your lenten observances.

Prayer

God of our conversion, lead us to sainthood through our lenten journey. May we embrace this time of penance in a spirit of prayer. May we fast from all that distracts us from you. May we come to the aid of those in need. At journey's end, may we find ourselves renewed as members of the body of Christ, in whose name we pray. Amen.

---

1. Thomas Merton, *The Seven Storey Mountain: An Autobiography of Faith* (New York: New Directions, 1948), p. 260.

· · · | · · ·

Thursday After Ash Wednesday

Thomas More: What Does It Profit Us?

Deuteronomy 30:15–20; Psalm 1:1–2, 3–4, 6; Luke 9:22–25

In the movie (based on the play by Robert Bolt) *A Man for All Seasons*, Sir Thomas More is on trial on trumped-up charges, having angered King Henry VIII, who had set himself up in place of the pope as head of the church in England.

A young protégé of More, Richard Rich, supports the king and commits perjury to give evidence that condemns More to death. Rich's reward for his treachery is appointment as attorney general for Wales. More looks at Rich and asks, "Why, Richard, it profits a man nothing to give his soul for the whole world…. But for Wales?" In today's Gospel, Luke gives the source of the line More is quoting, as Jesus declares: "What does it profit them if they gain the whole world, but lose or forfeit themselves?" (9:25).

Thomas More was a scholar, author, lawyer, family man, and chancellor of England. His intense spiritual convictions led him to oppose Henry's divorce and break with Rome. More's choice led to his death as a martyr in 1535.

Thomas More's courage and convictions offer us inspiration as Lent begins to work with the grace of God over forty days, remain focused on who we are as followers of Christ, withstand the world's distractions, and make the "man for all seasons" a great role model to follow.

Today's Action
How are you being challenged to conversion during this Lent? List one or two of your greatest temptations.

Prayer
God of our self-denial, show us how to embrace the cross of Jesus. Give us the wisdom to reorder our priorities so that we might gain eternal life. Amen.

Friday After Ash Wednesday

Sharbel Makhluf: Fasting With a Purpose

Isaiah 58:1–9a; Psalm 51:3–4, 5–6ab, 18–19; Matthew 9:14–15

Fasting is one of the three traditional ways to observe Lent (prayer and almsgiving are the other two), based on Jesus' description of them in our Ash Wednesday Gospel.

Today the Scripture readings focus on fasting. The prophet Isaiah chides the people for their behavior on fast days, pursuing evil and not God's ways. The Lord wants works of justice and compassion connected with fast days. In the Gospel, Jesus explains to the followers of John the Baptist that while he (Jesus) is with his disciples, they will not fast; only after he has left them will they fast.

Sharbel Makhluf was known for both his fasting *and* his care for those who sought him out for prayer and blessing. Born in a tiny village in Lebanon, he lived as a hermit in the second half of the nineteenth century, in connection with the Monastery of Saint Maron in Annaya, Lebanon. While maintaining his hermit life, he did occasionally bring the sacraments to villagers near the monastery. After his death at age seventy, his tomb became a destination for pilgrims seeking healing.

St. Sharbel is revered in both the Maronite and Roman rites. He offers us guidance for our lenten fasting as it is combined with both prayer and works of charity.

Today's Action
Consider some kind of fasting as a lenten practice—but make sure it leads you to a deeper awareness of and charity toward those in need.

Prayer
God of our fasting, show us how our hunger unites us with those in need of bread, how letting go of life's comforts can aid those lacking necessities for life. Amen.

Saturday After Ash Wednesday

Levi (Matthew) the Tax Collector:
Sinners Are Welcome

ISAIAH 58:9B–14; PSALM 86:1–2, 3–4, 5–6; LUKE 5:27–32

Luke—and Mark—tell us the story of Levi, a tax collector whom Jesus calls as a follower in today's Gospel passage. Levi promptly throws a party for Jesus. More tax collectors and others show up as well, prompting criticism from the Pharisees and scribes. Their disapproval draws one of Jesus' most important responses: "Those who are well have no need of a physician, but those who are sick; I have come to call not the righteous but sinners to repentance" (Luke 5:31–32).

Why did Levi not get numbered among the disciples of Jesus whose stories are told in the Gospel, such as Peter, Andrew, James, and John? We don't know. In Matthew's Gospel the evangelist (who was probably not the apostle Matthew) borrowed the story from Mark and changed Levi's name to "Matthew." Scholars suggest that the evangelist possibly wanted to match up this dramatic story of the conversion of a tax collector with "Matthew, the tax collector" who appears in all the listings of apostles.

This bit of biblical trivia is less important than the lesson Jesus gives. The Gospels are full of stories where Jesus meets and dines with sinners. In doing so, he overturned the expectations of "religious" people and proclaimed the reign of God through mercy and forgiveness. We are welcome in the company of Jesus, even though we are sinners.

Today's Action
When in your life have you been called by Jesus to follow him? Recall your own vocation story.

Prayer
God of forgiveness, surprise us today with the call to a change of heart. May we hear the voice of Jesus inviting us to follow him. Amen.

First Sunday of Lent

Noah: A Creation Covenant

Year A: Genesis 2:7–9, 3:1–7; Psalm 51:3–4, 5–6, 12–13, 17;
Romans 5:12–19; Matthew 4:1–11
Year B: Genesis 9:8–15; Psalm 25:4–5, 6–7, 8–9;
1 Peter 3:18–22; Mark 1:12–15
Year C: Deuteronomy 26:4–10; Psalm 91:1–2, 10–11,
12–13, 14–15; Romans 10:8–13; Luke 4:1–13

Author's Note: The Old Testament readings for the lenten Sundays in all three cycles present the history of salvation, one of the teaching themes of Lent. I've chosen a figure from the Old Testament for several of these Sundays to assist you in your lenten prayer.

We can't help but look at Noah through the lens of our modern sense of what's acceptable behavior. Building an ark in your neighborhood is probably not calculated to win the approval of your neighbors. Comedian Bill Cosby, as well as the film *Evan Almighty,* saw the potential for humor in the story of Noah.

In reality, though, Noah's response to God's call is seen by the scriptural text as an act of faith. The risk Noah took, whatever his neighbors thought about his strange building project, made possible the display of God's care for Noah and his family. It also helped introduce the biblical theme of covenant.

Following the flood, God makes a promise never to destroy his creation again by a flood (apocalyptic filmmakers, take note!). God's promise takes the form of a "covenant," a promise on God's part, which in turn calls forth a response on the part of humanity. Creation on God's part is an act of love, and the covenant with Noah reinforces that love.

The notion of covenant will surface again and again, until we hear it at the Last Supper. Jesus will offer us his Blood, poured out in a new covenant of love, helping to make each of us a new creation in Christ.

Today's Action
Step out today to observe God's creation and make your own covenant response to help protect that creation.

Prayer
God of the covenant, stretch your rainbow above us as a sign of your faithfulness. In the beauty of creation may we see your love written large and make a response of faith, with your help. Amen.

Monday of the First Week of Lent

Frances of Rome: When You Did for the Least Ones

LEVITICUS 19:1–2, 11–18 ; PSALM 19:8, 9,10, 15; MATTHEW 25:31–46

The first days of Lent feature scriptural selections that emphasize the lenten practices of prayer, fasting, and almsgiving. Today Moses articulates the love of neighbor as part of God's law. The people's conduct is motivated by the holiness of the God they worship. Jesus makes that motivation even more personal, in the famous Matthew 25 passage, in which he identifies himself with the poor and needy to whom we should minister in the world.

Frances of Rome, in the fourteenth century, can easily be patron of our lenten almsgiving, as we seek the face of Jesus in hungry, naked, homeless, ill, or imprisoned people. Married to a wealthy young nobleman, Frances teamed up with her sister-in-law to help the poor, with their husbands' support. Frances balanced her charity with care for her family, but when a severe plague broke out in Italy and spread to the city of Rome, Frances turned all her possessions into alms for the suffering. After her two children died, she turned part of her home into a hospital.

Eventually, she received permission to found a society of women not bound to traditional vows of religious life, dedicated to serving the poor. After her husband's death, Frances went to live with the society she founded, spending the rest of her life in finding Christ in those she helped.

Today's Action
Choose some kind of lenten almsgiving that will involve you in hands-on service with the poor.

Prayer
Jesus, visible in our neighbor, show us your face in the hungry and thirsty, the naked and homeless, the prisoner and the stranger. Move us to action so we may fulfill the ancient law to love God and neighbor. Amen.

Tuesday of the First Week of Lent

Isidore the Farmer: Prayer in the Midst of Our Labors

ISAIAH 55:10–11; PSALM 34:4–5, 6–7, 16–17, 18–19; MATTHEW 6:7–15

An old joke defines a farmer as someone "outstanding in his field." St. Isidore the Farmer not only stood out for his work in tilling the soil but was also a deeply prayerful man.

Today's First Reading uses images familiar to farmers. Isaiah describes the fertility of the word of God, comparing its power to that of the rain and snow in watering the earth, allowing it to bear fruit, producing seed for the sower and bread for the hungry.

Isidore lived from 1070 to 1130 in the vicinity of Madrid, Spain, where he worked on the estate of a wealthy landowner. He was generous to the poor, helping to feed them, and sensitive to the care of beasts of burden. But it is his spirit of prayer that is remembered—whether rising early to pray in church or praying as he plowed his fields. He is honored today as patron of Madrid and of the U.S. Bishops' Rural Life Conference.

Legend has it that Isidore's coworkers grumbled when he was late for work because he had stayed in church praying; the tales go on to relate how angels then came to take up the slack in his work.

We may have trouble finding time this Lent to pray. Isidore can teach us that it's possible to find the time for prayer in the midst of a busy life.

Today's Action
Decide how you will make time to pray this Lent.

Prayer
Word enfleshed, be fertile and fruitful in us, that we may come to know how you reveal the Father, and come to fulfill the divine will on earth as it is in heaven. Amen.

· · · | · · ·

Wednesday of the First Week of Lent

Jonah: The Sign of God's Mercy

JONAH 3:1–10; PSALM 51:3–4, 12–13, 18–19; LUKE 11:29–32

Most of us know the story of Jonah and the whale. But today's readings give us the rest of the story.

Jonah's mission as a prophet was to deliver a warning from God to the pagan city of Nineveh; his watery adventure was part of his wish to *escape* that mission. God ensures that Jonah does deliver the message, and when he does the results are overwhelmingly positive. Sadly, Jonah cannot accept the mercy God shows in the face of the surprising repentance of a whole city— including the livestock. (Jonah's disappointment is related in another part of the biblical book not given in today's selection.)

The point of this delightful and humorous story is precisely the merciful response of God. (The gracious nature of that mercy is emphasized in the tale in the repentance of the Assyrians, one of the most dreaded nations of the ancient Near East.)

So often we find it difficult to understand how God can be God. God seems to be able to show mercy to people we'd rather not forgive or even tolerate. It was the same for the opponents of Jesus. They could not accept him and how he brought God's forgiveness.

As today's Gospel shows, God had yet another surprise—the "sign of Jonah" present in the life, death, and resurrection of Jesus.

Today's Action
List three people in your life you haven't yet forgiven for some slight or offense. Ask God to help you to forgive them.

Prayer
God of the prophets, pursue us until we are ready to accept your call. Then grace us to be bold in proclaiming your love and forgiveness in the world. Amen.

Thursday of the First Week of Lent
Queen Esther: A Royal Request
ESTHER C:12, 14–16, 23–25; PSALM 138:1–2AB, 2CDE–3, 7C–8;
MATTHEW 7:7–12

The tale of Queen Esther has all the elements of a great story. We can imagine her, the beautiful bride of a pagan king, ruler of Persia, reigning in a lavish Middle Eastern court. Into this scene of elegance and splendor comes a threat to Esther's kin—the Jewish people who are exiled in her land.

The drama, essential to any good story, develops as the king's advisor, Haman, is angered by the refusal of Esther's uncle, Mordecai, to bow down to Haman in the court. In revenge, Haman plots to destroy all the Jews in the land.

When Esther learns of the plot, she risks her life to go to the king, her husband, and plead on behalf of her people, after praying the prayer found in our First Reading. Her prayers, and her pleas to the king, are answered positively, and the Jews in Persia are saved.

The Gospel follows with the simple assurance given us by Jesus about *our* prayer. "Ask, and it will be given to

you; search and the door will be opened for you"
(Matthew 7:7). It's a promise based on a relationship,
the relationship of Jesus to his Father, a relationship that
we're invited to share.

Today's Action
Reflect on Jesus' words about how God, our loving par-
ent, treats us. Then write a prayer of petition for some
special need.

Prayer
Generous Father, may we believe what Jesus has told us
about your willingness to hear our prayer. May we never
fear to ask, seek, and knock, confident in your love.
Amen.

· · · | · · ·

Friday of the First Week of Lent
Cornelius and Cyprian: Reconcilers in the Ancient Church
EZEKIEL 18:21–28; PSALM 130:1–2, 3–4, 5–7A, 7BC–8;
MATTHEW 5:20–26

The church has always been in need of reconciliation. Our human nature means that there will always be a need to forgive each other. Today's Gospel offers us Jesus' guidelines for forgiveness in the community. Matthew's "parish," the communities for whom he wrote, must have needed those guidelines—no surprise there. We're fortunate to have Jesus' instructions on how to be a reconciling community.

Sts. Cornelius and Cyprian faced one of the early church's thorniest problems. In the third century they wrestled with the problem of how to deal with Christians who had renounced their faith and sacrificed to idols in a time of persecution. Were they to be readmitted to the sacraments?

Cyprian, a bishop in North Africa, held to a moderate solution—welcome such sinners back at the time of death. He countered a priest who advocated a "free pass" for all, without any penance imposed.

Pope Cornelius, at the same time, had to deal with a priest (later condemned as a heretic for his stance) who held that the church could not reconcile any serious sinners—apostates, murderers, adulterers, and more. Together, these two church leaders, themselves later martyred for the faith, gave practical shape to Jesus' teaching on reconciliation.

In every age, the church must deal with issues not expressed by Jesus, but his gospel of mercy guides us still.

Today's Action
Pray for reconciliation in your family, parish, or neighborhood.

Prayer
God of second chances, help us to respond to your promise of life. And when we are forgiven, help us extend the same gift to those who sin against us. Amen.

Saturday of the First Week of Lent

Pio of Pietrelcina (Padre Pio): Signed With Christ's Love

DEUTERONOMY 26:16–19; PSALM 119:1–2, 4–5, 7–8; MATTHEW 5:43–48

Padre Pio was spiritual inspiration for the older Italian members of my family. He was for that generation what Mother Teresa is to mine. I recall reading stories and seeing photos of Padre Pio in the Italian religious magazines my Nonna received, and hearing from my cousin in Italy of a visit to the saint's shrine after his canonization.

Francesco Forgione entered the Capuchin Franciscans as a teenager. He received the name Pio and was ordained in 1910. In 1918, praying after Mass, Fr. Pio saw Jesus in a vision and afterward saw that he had received the wounds of Christ—the stigmata—in his hands, feet, and side.

His condition, like that of all modern stigmatics, was a cause for caution among his superiors, and Pio had to endure investigations by doctors and church officials. When he was at last allowed to do public ministry, his Masses and long hours in the confessional drew hundreds each day. He also was known for physical and spiritual healings worked through him.

Padre Pio knew many trials, but he understood that God's grace and love were available to all. He helped mediate that love and forgiveness through years of ministry, until his death in 1968. His bearing of the wounds of Christ reminds those entering the church this Lent that they are to identify completely with our Lord. Padre Pio understood, in the words of today's Gospel, how to "be perfect … as your heavenly Father is perfect" (Matthew 5:48).

Today's Action
Consider how God's covenant of love (today's First Reading) with us in Jesus is made visible in your life.

Prayer
God, who gave the Law to Moses, teach us the Law's perfection in Jesus. Show us how to be merciful to enemies and to love those who hate us. In imitation of Jesus, may we embrace the sinner and forgive those who do us harm. Amen.

• • • | • • •

Second Sunday of Lent

Abraham: A Legacy of Faith

Year A: Genesis 12:1–4a; Psalm 33:4–5, 18–19, 20, 22;
2 Timothy 1:8–10; Matthew 17:1–9

Year B: Genesis 22:1–2, 9a, 10–13, 15–18; Psalm 116:10, 15, 16–17,
18–19; Romans 8:31b–34, Mark 9:2–10

Year C: Genesis 15:5–12, 17–18; Psalm 27:1, 7–8a, 8b–9, 13–14;
Philippians 3:17—4:1; Luke 9:28b–36

In Lent we read stories about Abraham—the description of God's covenant with him and the story of his willingness to sacrifice his son Isaac, for example. These stories have undergone a long process of telling and retelling. Many hands have worked over these stories, for theological purposes.

Nevertheless, the stories communicate the common understanding we share about Abraham; that is, his strong faith in God. We marvel at this man's willingness to trust in God so much that he would undertake a long, difficult journey to seek a land and a heritage promised by God. Though separated by millennia and by different cultures, we are yet the children of Abraham.

In John's Gospel, Jesus confronts his opponents who claim that inheritance but fail to go beyond paying lip-service to it. Lent is all about renewing our faith in God through Jesus Christ, his Son.

May we use our lenten immersion in the stories of faith as opportunities to allow God to strengthen and challenge that faith, as God did for Abraham. May we share our stories of faith with those entering the church this season.

Today's Action
Visit a local mosque during Lent and ask about the stories and figures we share with Muslims. If there isn't a mosque nearby, read about Islam and learn more about these connections.

Prayer
All-merciful God, worshiped by the People of the Book, may we imitate our father Abraham in fidelity, trusting where you would lead us. Amen.

Monday of the Second Week of Lent

John Vianney: Ministering God's Forgiveness

DANIEL 9:4B–10; PSALM 79:8, 9, 11, 13; LUKE 6:36–38

Confession of sin is the theme of our First Reading today, as the people of God confess their disobedience to the Lord and seek God's forgiveness. Conversion and confession remain a powerful lenten theme. Parishes celebrate the sacrament of reconciliation in communal liturgies during this season, and our lenten practices are meant to inspire us in our ongoing conversion.

The saint best known for his ministry in the sacrament of reconciliation is John Vianney, who was ordained in 1815 in France, after years of study that were interrupted by seminary officials who thought him inadequate for the priesthood as well as by political upheaval. The French Revolution had wreaked havoc with the church, and in his first and only pastorate, the small town of Ars, Vianney found ignorance and great spiritual need.

He lived a rigorous life of prayer and fasting and devoted himself to the pastoral care of his people, primarily through the confessional. In time, his fame spread throughout the world. Eventually, Fr. Vianney was hearing confessions for eleven to twelve hours in winter and sixteen hours in the summer. His few hours of sleep at night were often interrupted by the devil. By 1855, four years before his death at age seventy-three, more than twenty thousand pilgrims a year were coming to Ars.

In our day the long lines at the confessional have dwindled in many places, although communal penance services attract many parishioners during Advent and Lent. May St. John Vianney's life and dedication to this sacrament inspire us to rediscover its power in our own lives.

Today's Action
Make plans to participate in your parish's communal celebration of the sacrament of reconciliation, or go to individual confession at least once this season.

Prayer
God of the covenant, we come to you in our sinfulness. Open us to your grace and help us accept your forgiveness. Amen.

Tuesday of the Second Week of Lent

Thérèse of the Child Jesus: Service in Humility

Isaiah 1:10, 16–20; Psalm 50:8–9, 16bc–17, 21, 23; Matthew 23:1–12

Priests get asked occasionally—usually by folks of a fundamentalist Christian bent—about today's Gospel text, in which Jesus tells us we should not use the title *father* for anyone on earth—only for our Father in heaven. Leaving aside the question of what they might call their own dads, they are missing the point of Jesus' words, which come at the end of the passage: "The greatest among you must be your servant. All who exalt themselves will be humbled, and all who humble themselves will be exalted" (Matthew 23:11–12).

We are not to use titles but rather serve in humility. A saint who embodied that ideal bore the religious name Thérèse of the Child Jesus; tradition has given her a title befitting her humility, "the Little Flower." She became a Carmelite nun in Lisieux, France, in 1888 at age fifteen, and died just nine years later. Her life in the convent was spent in prayer and arduous manual work that taxed her already frail frame, weakened by childhood illness.

Though she did not seek fame, Thérèse's autobiography, *The Story of a Soul*, has become a spiritual classic, and her influence as a teacher of holiness led to her being named a doctor of the church in 1997.

The Little Flower is a good patron for our lenten walk with Jesus. His words about humble service are meant for all who would become his followers.

Today's Action
Reflect on what humility means in your life.

Prayer
Jesus, teach us humility. May our lenten self-denial move us to serve others in imitation of the Little Flower. Amen.

• • • | • • •

Wednesday of the Second Week of Lent
James and John: From Arrogance to Witness
<small>JEREMIAH 18:18–20; PSALM 31:5–6, 14, 15–16; MATTHEW 20:17–28</small>

To read today's Gospel, one would think that Jesus'
apostles could have really used a public-relations advisor! The story of the mother of James and John,
requesting places for her sons at Jesus' right and left
hands in his kingdom, does not reflect well on these
followers of the Lord. What makes it worse, Jesus has
just predicted his passion and death. Were they even
listening?

At least, the arrogant request gives Jesus the opportunity to challenge James and John to share in his sufferings. He goes on to urge his followers not to imitate the
gentile rulers and their hangers-on. Instead, they are to
seek to serve if they want to rank first in the kingdom.

Why did the early church retell this and other stories
that show Jesus' disciples as slow to understand him and
even cowardly in the face of his arrest, trial, and death?
Perhaps one reason is that the tradition remembered
these stories, and the evangelists worked them into their
narrative to show the humanness of the church at its
very beginning.

God's power was certainly at work from the start. Jesus' resurrection and the gift of his Holy Spirit transformed these first followers into witnesses. Jesus remains with the church until the end of time, strengthening it, forgiving the sins of its leaders and faithful, and continuing to offer the way of the cross as our way to humble service and salvation.

Today's Action
Pick an opportunity to be of service to someone today, even if only within your own family or at work.

Prayer
Suffering Lord, may we walk with you on the way of the cross. Strengthen us to let go of selfish ambition and join you in serving others. Amen.

Thursday of the Second Week of Lent

André Bessette: The Doorkeeper Saint

JEREMIAH 17:5–10; PSALM 1:1–2, 3, 4, 6; LUKE 16:19–31

Jesus tells the parable of a rich man who lived in luxury, failing to notice the beggar named Lazarus at his front door. Only too late—after death—does the rich man take notice of the poor man who had daily suffered on his doorstep.

The French Canadian saint André Bessette would not have been blind to a beggar on his doorstep. After twenty-five years of struggle with sickness and poverty, and having tried various trades, including working in a New England factory during the Civil War, he joined the Congregation of Holy Cross in Montreal in 1872. Weak health had delayed his profession, and he was assigned the job of doorkeeper. He joked much later in life that when he entered religious life, he was shown the door and remained there for forty years.

Brother André had a rich spiritual life, fed by long hours of prayer. He visited the sick and brought oil from the chapel lamp to apply to them. Soon reports of healings began to spread. Such notoriety made his religious order and church authorities nervous; Brother André adamantly deferred any personal powers, claiming instead the intercession of St. Joseph. He was instrumental in building a shrine to St. Joseph on Mount Royal. It became a place of pilgrimage where many miracles of healing are claimed.

Humble Brother André would have felt a kinship with the beggar Lazarus at the rich man's door. He died in 1937 at age ninety-one and was canonized in 2010.

Today's Action
Visit, send a card, or make a phone call to someone who is sick within your family or your parish or among your friends.

Prayer
Jesus, may we hear you knocking on the door of our heart. Through the intercession of your foster father, Joseph, may all who suffer find healing and peace. Amen.

Friday of the Second Week of Lent

The Patriarch Joseph: A Story of a Dreamer

GENESIS 37:3–4, 12–13A, 17B–28A; PSALM 105:16–17, 18–19, 20–21;
MATTHEW 21:33–43, 45–46

Two biblical characters are the subject of Broadway musicals by composer Andrew Lloyd Webber, and both are featured in today's readings. They are Joseph, the son of Israel (Jacob) in Genesis, and Jesus, the "superstar" of Matthew's Gospel! Webber seized on the detail of Joseph's coat (here simply a "long tunic") as the launch point for one musical. But there's much in the Joseph story to entertain.

Joseph the dreamer is the victim of violence at the hands of his jealous brothers. He goes on to have interesting adventures in Egypt and rises to become Pharaoh's adviser in a time of famine. The story ends happily as Joseph helps to save his family and is reunited with them.

Jesus' story, as prefigured in a parable Jesus tells to his opponents in today's Gospel, parallels that of Joseph. In the story, the son of a property owner is murdered by the hired hands. It is a clear message to Jesus' enemies that they had placed themselves in opposition to God. Their plot against Jesus will, in the end, find them disinherited.

Matthew was a great storyteller. He drew on the Joseph in Genesis to enrich his portrait of the Joseph in the infancy story with which Matthew began his Gospel. There, another Joseph dreams, goes to Egypt, and protects the child in his care, who will grow up to save his people.

Today's Action
Listen to a selection from the musical *Joseph and the Amazing Technicolor Dreamcoat*, or read the Genesis citation from today's First Reading. Reflect on the power of the biblical story to lead us to a deeper understanding of God.

Prayer
God of the patriarchs, fill us with the power of the great stories of our faith. May we find our own stories in the pages of salvation history. Amen.

Saturday of the Second Week of Lent

Augustine: The Grace of Conversion
Micah 7:14–15, 18–20; Psalm 103:1–2, 3–4, 9–10, 11–12;
Luke 15:1–3, 11–32

The story of the Prodigal Son in Luke's Gospel personifies the mercy of God. Many commentators and homilists suggest the story is mistitled and think it should be called "The Father Who Couldn't Forget." The father, who is spurned by a selfish, insensitive son who squanders his share of the family fortune, suffers not only personal shame but public embarrassment as his close-knit community watches him wait daily for his son's return.

The story of St. Augustine is, in part, the story of a *mother* who couldn't forget.

A talented and scholarly young man, Augustine immersed himself in all the shallow pursuits of his pagan society. His mother, Monica, never gave up in praying for his conversion, even following him from North Africa to Rome and on to Milan. There, Augustine met Bishop Ambrose, whose influence, along with Augustine's search of the Scriptures, were key to his embrace of Christianity.

Baptized in 387, Augustine was ordained a priest three years later and became bishop of Hippo, in North Africa, in 395. His writings, such as his *Confessions* and *The City of God*, are spiritual classics. His philosophy and theology have influenced the church until the present day.

But for our lenten journey, the inspiration of a mother's prayer, God's grace of conversion, and the response of a sinner are the most important lessons we learn from the life of St. Augustine.

Today's Action
Is there someone in your family or community in need of God's grace of conversion? Pray for that person today.

Prayer
Good Shepherd, seek us out when we are lost. Call our name, and we will hear your voice and respond. Lead us to green pastures. Amen.

Third Sunday of Lent

Moses: Knowing We Are God's People

YEAR A: EXODUS 17:3–7; PSALM 95:1–2, 6–7, 8–9;
ROMANS 5:1–2, 5–8; JOHN 4:5–42
YEAR B: EXODUS 20:1–17; PSALM 19:8, 9, 10, 11;
1 CORINTHIANS 1:22–25; JOHN 2:13–25
YEAR C: EXODUS 3:1–8A, 13–15; PSALM 103:1–2, 3–4, 6–7, 8, 11;
1 CORINTHIANS 10:1–6, 10–12; LUKE 13:1–9

The character of Moses is forever burned into the consciousness of a generation of moviegoers by Charlton Heston's portrayal of him in *The Ten Commandments*. Moses strides through the film, leading his people out of Egypt, stretching his staff over a divided Red Sea, and bringing the tablets of the Law down from his encounter with God on the mountain.

We hear about many different dimensions of Moses in lenten readings drawn from the books of Exodus and Deuteronomy, and Moses returns the favor in a passage read on the first Sunday of Lent in the C Cycle of readings. In describing the ritual for offering first fruits from the harvest of the Promised Land, Moses says that the people must describe themselves thusly: "A wandering Aramean was my ancestor; he went down into Egypt and lived there as an alien" (Deuteronomy 26:5). He goes on to retell the story of the liberation of the Hebrew people from Egypt by God's "mighty hand and an outstretched arm" (8). God has now settled the people in the Promised Land. As they enjoy the blessings of God's covenant, they make an offering to remind themselves who has given them those blessings.

Lent is when we bring people to a new identity in Christ through baptism. Those already baptized renew that identity. Following Moses' example, may we use this time to recall what God has done for us in Jesus.

Today's Action
As a lenten activity, outline your family's religious history and your place in it.

Prayer
God who names us as your people, never let us forget your mighty deeds on our behalf. Bring those seeking baptism to life in you. For the rest of us, renew our identity in Jesus, as his body, the church, in the world. Amen.

• • • | • • •

Monday of the Third Week of Lent
Damien Joseph de Veuster of Molokai:
A Mission Among the Lepers

2 Kings 5:1–15a; Psalm 42:2–3; 43:3–4; Luke 4:24–30

Leprosy is a disease that gets a lot of attention in the
Bible. Jesus, who himself healed lepers, cites the story of
the cure of the Syrian leper, Naaman, in today's Gospel,
as he challenges his hometown audience with the rejec-
tion of prophets in their native place, while foreigners
like Naaman receive God's favor.

In modern times leprosy, or Hansen's disease, is treat-
able, but at the time of St. Damien of Molokai it was still
feared. Those suffering from the disease were kept as far
as possible from others, as on the Hawaiian island of
Molokai, on a remote, inaccessible peninsula. It was
there that the Belgian missionary Damien came, fulfill-
ing a lifelong dream of mission work. Ordained in
Honolulu in 1864, he came to the leper colony nine
years later. At first part of a rotating team of chaplains,
he later settled into a permanent ministry there.

The story of the end of Damien's life is well known.
In 1884 he contracted leprosy himself, and could then

address his flock, "We lepers…." He died five years later, in 1889, and has been acclaimed in both Hawaii and in his native Belgium.

Damien teaches us, as Pope John Paul II declared at his beatification, that "holiness is not perfection according to human criteria; it is not reserved for a small number of exceptional persons. It is for everyone." This is a good thought to ponder throughout Lent.

Today's Action

Who are the "lepers" in your life? Plan some form of outreach to those you usually avoid.

Prayer

Healing God, do not let us shrink from those who may appear disfigured in body or troubled in spirit. Lead us among them and show us how to embrace them with love. Amen.

Note: In the third, fourth, and fifth weeks of Lent, in years other than Year A in the cycle of readings, the presider at weekday Mass may choose the Year A Gospel from John, of the woman at the well, the man born blind, or the raising of Lazarus, respectively.

Tuesday of the Third Week of Lent

Alphonsus Liguori: Gentle Moral Teacher

Daniel 3:25, 34–43; Psalm 25:4bc–5ab, 6, 7bc, 8–9; Matthew 18:21–35

In today's Gospel, Peter asks Jesus a question: How often should we forgive a brother who offends us? Peter suggests that perhaps seven times would be a generous offer. Scripture scholar Fr. Raymond Brown notes that, at this point, we who know Jesus' answer are inclined to criticize Peter. How stingy! We know Jesus is going to respond with a whopping seventy-seven times, suggesting forgiveness without limit.

But, Brown comments, who among us, realistically, might squeeze out a second or, just maybe, a third act of forgiveness? After that, wouldn't we say, "Enough!"? At that point, Brown says, Peter is looking pretty good! And that makes Jesus' rule for forgiveness even more generous. It is, in fact, the generosity of God.

In the eighteenth century, St. Alphonsus Liguori lived at a time when moral theology, the church's interpretation of human behavior and sin in light of the gospel, was wrestling with the rigid standards of a group called the Jansenists. Eventually they were condemned as heretics by the church because they denied the role of free will in the acceptance and use of grace. Alphonsus wrote a practical guide for pastors and confessors that was for centuries a standard text. It was marked by moderation and the attitude of forgiveness taught by Jesus in today's Gospel.

Alphonsus is honored as a doctor of the church for more than his moral theology. He was a great spiritual writer, founder of the Redemptorist Congregation, and a model of patient suffering in his personal life. But as we consider our own sinfulness and seek God's mercy, the kindness and gentleness that marked his moral teaching can inspire us to conversion.

Today's Action

Examine your conscience in light of the Ten Commandments and the Beatitudes.

Prayer

Jesus, teach us unlimited forgiveness, as you commanded Peter. May we never forget how many times we have been forgiven, and may we always be ready to show forgiveness to others. Amen.

$\bullet \ \bullet \ \bullet \ | \ \bullet \ \bullet \ \bullet$

Wednesday of the Third Week of Lent

Francis de Sales: From Lawyer to Spiritual Guide

Deuteronomy 4:1, 5–9; Psalm 147:12–13, 15–16, 19–20;
Matthew 5:17–19

When we think of Moses, we often think of the Ten Commandments, the laws that God gave to Israel. Today's First Reading offers an address by Moses to the people, in which he encourages them to observe the Law and thus witness to the nations of the greatness of their God.

In Matthew's Gospel, Jesus is portrayed as the "new Moses" as he teaches the Torah, the Law of Moses, in the Sermon on the Mount but expands it in light of the kingdom. Jesus offers ways in which the Law is to be enfleshed in love and mercy, even beyond what Moses taught.

St. Francis de Sales was marked by his family for a legal career, following in his father's footsteps as a distinguished jurist in France. After receiving legal training, however, Francis opted for the priesthood. In doing so, he became an interpreter of the Law of God as Jesus teaches it. His spiritual writings, especially his

Introduction to the Devout Life and *A Treatise on the Love of God*, are the best known among his many writings. They were meant for ordinary people, making it clear that anyone can become a saint, with God's help.

Francis' pastoral style graced not only his writing on the spiritual life but his service as a bishop as well. His own personal struggle with a fierce temper was informed by the meekness Jesus taught in the Beatitudes. Francis learned well how to translate the Law into the life Christ brings us.

Today's Action
Spend some time with a book of spiritual reading or inspiration.

Prayer
God, who gave the Law to Moses, help us not to forget how you led us through the wilderness and brought us to our home. Show us the way to teach others how Jesus fulfills the Law in love. Amen.

· · · | · · ·

Thursday of the Third Week of Lent
Patrick: The Struggle Against Evil
JEREMIAH 7:23–28; PSALM 95:1–2, 6–7, 8–9; LUKE 11:14–23

The popular book *The Rite,* which was later made into a movie, tells the story of a young priest who learns how to fight again the very real manifestation of the devil's power. Through prayer and the power of God mediated through the church's ritual of exorcism, people throughout the centuries have been delivered from the grip of evil.

Today's Gospel, from Luke, gives one of many episodes in the story of Jesus where he drives out a devil and brings relief to a person who has been possessed. In the process, Jesus describes the intensity of the struggle against evil. It was a struggle St. Patrick knew well. As the "apostle to Ireland" in the fifth century, he had to fight against the pagan religion that was entrenched there. His powerful preaching and energetic building of the church throughout the land helped to root Christianity in Ireland.

Exorcism is still needed today. The real cases described in *The Rite* are rare occurrences, but exorcism of a less dramatic nature occurs on the third, fourth, and fifth Sundays of Lent.

In the initiation ritual of the scrutinies, pastors pray a prayer of exorcism, which is meant to strengthen the candidates for baptism, living in a world where the power of evil is real. We are confident as we pray these prayers that the power of Jesus is with each of us in our struggle to be faithful.

Today's Action
Try to attend a Sunday Mass in your parish where the scrutinies are taking place as part of the Rite of Christian Initiation of Adults. Consider some of the instances where you have encountered evil in your own life.

Prayer
May we hear your voice clearly today, O God. Melt our stubborn hearts, and free us from the grip of evil. Amen.

• • • | • • •

Friday of the Third Week of Lent

Bl. Teresa of Calcutta: Longing for God With Our Whole Being

HOSEA 14:2–10; PSALM 8:6C–8A, 8BC-9, 10–11AB, 14, 17; MARK 12:28B–34

No list of lenten saints would be complete without Bl. Mother Teresa of Calcutta. I was fortunate enough to see her in person in June 1981. I didn't get to meet her personally but felt blessed just to be in her presence.

Little did we know that this saintly woman had, for many years, walked a path of inner darkness. Several years ago, Fr. Brian Kolodiejchuk, promoting her cause for sainthood, edited a book called *Mother Teresa: Come Be My Light.* He recalled the years she endured dark nights of the soul, despite her great love for God and certainty that God had called her to special work with the poor.

Fr. Kolodiejchuk says that "the paradoxical and totally unsuspected cost of her mission was that she herself would live in 'terrible darkness.'" She wrote her spiritual director in 1961 of "this terrible sense of loss— this untold darkness—this loneliness—this continual longing for God—which gives me that pain deep down in my heart…. The place of God in my soul is blank."[1]

I can't help but think back to the little, bent-over woman I saw that June day. We thought of her as a living saint, even then. Was she still walking in spiritual darkness?

Mother Teresa lived out the words of today's Gospel, to love God with all her being and her neighbor as herself. Her appeal to me—beyond all of the good she did—was that she never gave up longing for God, even in the "terrible darkness." It's not perfection in what we do that makes us saints, but allowing God to work with who we are.

Today's Action
Offer your times of uncertainty and darkness to God today.

Prayer
Lord, our God, may we worship you alone with all of our being. May we love our neighbor as ourselves and, in so doing, come close to your heavenly reign. Amen.

1. Brian Kolodiejchuk, *Mother Teresa: Come Be My Light: The Private Writings of the Saint of Calcutta* (New York: Doubleday, 2007), pp. 1–2.

· · · | · · ·

Saturday of the Third Week of Lent
Martin de Porres: The Humble Exalted
Hosea 6:1–6; Psalm 51:3–4, 18–19, 20–21ab; Luke 18:9–14

Picture the simple Dominican brother Martin de Porres moving humbly among the sick and poor of Lima, Peru, in the seventeenth century. His work was long and arduous as he cared for orphans, slaves, and poor children. His hours of prayer and penance strengthened this ministry. At first only a lay helper in this community, thinking himself unworthy to be a vowed religious, Martin was eventually invited into full membership. His life of prayer and witness moved the Dominican community to receive him as a lay brother.

Like the tax collector in today's Gospel, Martin himself was someone whom society rejected. As the illegitimate son of a Spanish nobleman and Panamanian woman of color, he was victimized by poverty and social stigma. And yet he ministered to all, regardless of social standing, race, or color. As a man of mixed race, he stood out as a witness to gospel love.

In our American society, which is scarred by what one historian calls the "original sin" of slavery, racism is a real and insidious force. We tiptoe around its presence in our lives and in our institutions, and yet we need not fear to face it with the liberating power of the gospel.

A saint like Martin de Porres can teach us much, as we make a resolution to overcome all prejudice and racism and incorporate this into our lenten prayer.

Today's Action

Spend some time doing an honest examination of how your life might be touched by racism—whether in yourself or in others.

Prayer

God of love, draw us back to you. Rain down your love on our barren hearts and bring them to life. Amen.

· · · | · · ·
Fourth Sunday of Lent
Paul: Helping to Shape Our Christian Identity
Year A: 1 Samuel 16:1b, 6–7, 10–13; Psalm 23:1–3a, 3b–4, 5, 6;
Ephesians 5:8–14; John 9:1–41
Year B: 2 Chronicles 36:14–16, 19–23; Psalm 137:1–2, 3, 4–5, 6;
Ephesians 2:4–10; John 3:14–21
Year C: Joshua 5:9a, 10–12: Psalm 34:2–3, 4–5, 6–7; 2 Corinthians
5:17–21; Luke 15:1–3, 11–32

Old Testament readings take priority in Lent. Most of
the First Readings on weekdays are from the Hebrew
Scriptures; the First Reading each Sunday is chosen to
recall the story of salvation. The writings of St. Paul,
however, also appear on the Sundays of Lent. As I was
trying to find a place in this book for the Apostle to the
Gentiles, a friend reminded me of how Paul bridges the
Old and New Testaments. His theology helps to shape
much of our Christian identity.

Paul bookends Lent with his themes. On Ash
Wednesday, we read Paul quoting Isaiah, "'At an acceptable time I have listened to you, / and on a day of salvation I have helped you'" (2 Corinthians 6:2). This passage has always heralded for me the start of the lenten
journey of penance and conversion.

As we celebrate Palm Sunday, we hear (in all three cycles) Paul's great hymn of "emptying" from Philippians. He reminds us: "Let the same mind be in you that was in Christ Jesus, / who, though he was in the form of God, / did not regard equality with God / as something to be exploited, but emptied himself, / taking the form of a slave, / being born in human likeness / (Philippians 2:6–7).

This total emptying of the Incarnation, this poverty of God, inspired so many saints, including Francis of Assisi. It is how we are to identify with Christ, Paul tells us. And he goes on to describe Christ's total obedience in his death on a cross, the destination and climax of our lenten journey, leading to resurrection and glory.

Today's Action
Study one of Paul's letters in its entirety as a lenten prayer and reflection.

Prayer
Jesus, may our attitude be yours. Help us to let go of all that keeps us from life with you. May today for us be a day of salvation. Amen.

Monday of the Fourth Week of Lent

John the Evangelist: Jesus' Identity and Mission

Isaiah 65:17–21; Psalm 30:2, 4, 5–6, 11–12a, 13b; John 4:43–54

Today begins a semi-continuous reading of the Gospel of John. The organizers of the *Roman Catholic Lectionary for Mass* wanted to present a healthy portion of the fourth Gospel, to help us appreciate its richness. The sequence of texts also helps us focus on the person of Jesus and his mission.

John's Gospel is at once profound and elegantly simple. From its opening words announcing the Word made flesh, to the accounts of the signs of Jesus (such as today's cure of a royal official's son), to the three great scrutiny Gospels used in the rite of adult initiation, to the majestic Passion narrative, the fourth Gospel offers us a portrait of Jesus uniquely different from those of Matthew, Mark, and Luke.

The Gospel, in its simplest terms, shows us how Jesus has come to reveal the Father. In our lenten selections, that mission is presented in great dialogues between Jesus and his opponents.

(The term "Jews," used throughout these dialogues, reflects hostility between Christians and the Jewish synagogue near the end of the first century, not meant to foster anti-Semitic reading of the text into our time.)

We'll hear those dialogues over the next two weeks, cast in a kind of courtroom drama. Jesus testifies to his identity and mission. His opponents are frustrated as Jesus presents evidence of the works he has performed in doing his Father's will. He calls Abraham as a witness and claims identity with God in the divine name, I AM.

In a season that asks us to scrutinize our Christian identity in preparation for the celebration of baptism and renewal of our commitment to Christ, John's Gospel is an ideal companion for prayer and reflection.

Today's Action
Take time to read an introduction to the Gospel of John in your Bible or in a Scripture commentary.

Prayer
Word Made Flesh, show us the Father. May we accept your truth and come to have life in you! Amen.

· · · | · · ·

Tuesday of the Fourth Week of Lent

Ezekiel: Prophet of Liturgy and Rebirth

EZEKIEL 47:1–9, 12; PSALM 46:2–3, 5–6, 8–9; JOHN 5:1–3A, 5–16

When there are people to be baptized in my parish during Lent, the whole season takes on a different character. Everything leads to the waters of the font.

The conclusion of the catechumens' journey through the lenten season focuses their final preparation for the Easter sacraments. We hear the Scriptures at Mass through the filter of those entering the church. We celebrate rituals—large and small—with the Sunday community and in the circle of candidates and sponsors.

But in the end, we come to the waters of the font. To help us in "sighting" our destination, today's liturgy offers us a beautiful reading from the prophet Ezekiel. His book is full of wonderful, symbolic imagery, for example, the dry bones and the wheel of fire. He was a priest as well as a prophet, and so has a unique concern for the temple and its liturgy. He might be a special patron for those of us working with the liturgies of this season! He worked during the time of the exile in Babylon, sharing the lot of those taken there in 597. He prophesied the destruction of Jerusalem ten years later. He looked forward to a rebirth of Israel, and his promise of a new covenant would be realized in Jesus.

Today's passage of the water flowing from the Temple, beginning as a trickle and becoming a mighty river that brings healing and fruitfulness, is a perfect complement to Jesus' cure of a man by Jerusalem's Pool of Bethesda. And the prophet gives us a preview of the liturgy of the Easter Vigil, when we celebrate the initiation sacraments of baptism, confirmation, and Eucharist for those becoming Christian.

Today's Action
Place a bowl of water and a spring plant on your table today.

Prayer
God, we seek the life-giving waters of Easter, there to be cleansed and renewed and brought to new life in Christ. Amen.

· · · | · · ·

Wednesday of the Fourth Week of Lent

Gianna Beretta Molla: A Mother's Total Offering

Isaiah 49:8–15; Psalm 145:8–9, 13cd–14, 17–18; John 5:17–30

One of the most affectionate lines in all of Scripture occurs in our First Reading today: "Can a mother forget her nursing child, / or show no compassion for the child of her womb? / Even these may forget, / yet I will not forget you" (Isaiah 49:15).

The beautiful comparison of God's love to that of a mother for her child is captured in the life of St. Gianna Beretta Molla. Born in northern Italy in 1925, she pursued a career in medicine and became a physician and surgeon.

Gianna and her husband Peter had three children. While pregnant with her fourth child, Gianna was told she had a uterine tumor. Among the options offered by her doctors was a complete hysterectomy or an abortion. Gianna refused to terminate the pregnancy. She chose instead to have the tumor removed, despite the risk to her own health.

Gianna observed before undergoing surgery, "I have entrusted myself to the Lord in faith and hope.... I trust in God, yes, but now I must fulfill my duty as a mother. I renew the offer of my life to the Lord. I am ready for everything, provided the life of my child is saved."[1]

Gianna's priority, even as the pregnancy threatened her own life, was the life of her child. The infant, Gianna Emanuela, was born April 21, 1962. Mother Gianna struggled for seven days with severe pain and serious infection and died on April 28. The second miracle attesting to her cause for canonization was the healthy delivery of a baby to a mother whose own pregnancy was threatened at sixteen weeks.

Gianna's life and death offers us a powerful image in itself of the intimate love of God for us.

Today's Action
Offer your gift of time to Birthright or other organizations that support unborn life.

Prayer
God of life, help us to respect life in all its wondrous appearances in our life. May we defend and preserve life where it is threatened. Amen.

---

1. As quoted by Susan Hines-Brigger in "Saint for Moms and Everyday People" in *St. Anthony Messenger,* April 2007.

• • • | • • •

Thursday of the Fourth Week of Lent

Anthony of Padua: The Hammer of Heretics

Exodus 32:7–14; Psalm 106:19–20, 21–22, 23; John 5:31–47

Before he became the "go-to" saint for finding lost objects, St. Anthony of Padua had another nickname: "The Hammer of Heretics."

A contemporary of St. Francis of Assisi, Anthony was one of the first scholars of the Franciscan movement, appointed as a teacher of theology yet combining learning with holiness. Anthony put those talents to use as a great popular preacher. It wasn't his first choice. He had hoped to be a martyr, inspired by the first Franciscan martyrs whose bodies he saw in his native Portugal in 1220 when they were brought back from Morocco. That experience led him to join the Order and seek a similar fate.

Anthony's wish soon came to pass and he headed to North Africa, but poor health shortened his stay in Morocco. He eventually ended up in Italy at a great gathering of friars in 1221, where he met Francis. A year later, Anthony was attending an ordination ceremony where he was called on to preach when others declined.

His sermon showed that he had a preacher's gifts. These were put to use throughout Italy and France, as Anthony combated heresies and helped to reconcile them with the church. His work continued until a few months before his death in 1231.

In today's Gospel, Jesus confronts those determined to kill him and his message. He boldly proclaims the truth of who he is and where he has come from. Anthony learned from the Lord and helped many find faith in him.

Today's Action

Ask Anthony to help you find a deeper faith in the final weeks of Lent.

Prayer

God, whom we worship in awe, make us your people and let us journey with you. May we accept your Son's truth and come to know him and so possess life eternal. Amen.

• • • | • • •

Friday of the Fourth Week of Lent

Ignatius of Loyola: A Soldier's Spiritual Conflict
WISDOM 2:1A, 12–22; PSALM 34:17–18, 19–20, 21, 23; JOHN 7:1–2, 10, 25–30

"You know me, and you know where I am from. I have not come on my own. But the one who sent me is true, and you do not know him. I know him, because I am from him, and he sent me" (John 7:28–29). These words are from today's Gospel of John, as Jesus, threatened by his enemies, nevertheless comes to the Temple in Jerusalem for the Feast of Tabernacles. He begins to teach openly about who he is. His words challenge those who would claim intimacy with God but are in fact far from it.

In this second part of Lent, we focus more sharply on who Jesus is and how his identity and mission clash with the world. This conflict will surface in passages from John over the next weeks.

St. Ignatius of Loyola was no stranger to conflict. He was a soldier, wounded in battle. During his recovery he began to read about the lives of Christ and the saints. His conversion began in a personal faith struggle that

61

tested his growing intimacy with God. From that struggle, he wrote his classic *Spiritual Exercises,* which seekers and believers use to this day. From the crucible of his own spiritual conflict came his vocation: He and six companions began the Society of Jesus in 1534.

Tested over time, the Jesuit charism remains today true to the obedience and loyalty to the church that soldier Ignatius rooted in the Society. From it, we can draw inspiration in our lenten effort to better know who Jesus is, where he came from, and what his mission is.

Today's Action
Read a book by a Jesuit author, such as Fr. James Martin's *The Jesuit Guide to (Almost) Everything: A Spirituality for Real Life* for a taste of Jesuit spirituality, or go to the website www.sacredspace.ie, a ministry of the Irish Jesuits.

Prayer
Jesus, help us know you. In knowing you, may we also come to know the One who sent you. Amen.

Saturday of the Fourth Week of Lent

Teresa of Avila: A Woman for More Than Her Time

JEREMIAH 11;18–20; PSALM 7:2–3, 9BC–10, 11–12; JOHN 7:40–53

In the classic *Saint of the Day: Lives, Lessons, and Feasts*, which I used alongside the lectionary in preparing these reflections, there's a great description of St. Teresa of Avila: "Like Jesus, she was a mystery of paradoxes: wise, yet practical; intelligent, yet much in tune with her experience; mystic, yet an energetic reformer. A holy woman, a womanly woman."[1]

The lectionary readings continue to give us the sense of the growing plot against Jesus. Today we hear a snippet from the plot against the prophet Jeremiah, then we listen to discussions about whether Jesus is the Messiah. The chief priests and Pharisees debate this as well, and a dissenter, Nicodemus, offers support for Jesus.

Against the backdrop of such tension, Teresa seems an ideal guide. She lived in the turbulent sixteenth century, when the world was being shaken by the discoveries of explorers from Europe. In society, intellectual debate stirred the pot, and in the church, the Protestant

Reformation and the impact of the Council of Trent made this an age of upheaval.

Teresa brought her prodigious gifts to her time. She grounded her public persona in a deep personal life. As a woman, she was able to hold her own against opposition. Within her Carmelite Order, she was a reformer who brought change through her writing and speaking.

Teresa might find herself at home in our contemporary world and church. Her talents—recognized by her being named a doctor of the church in 1970—would serve us well as we continue to come to know Jesus.

Today's Action

Read about Teresa's life or some of her spiritual writings.

Prayer

When our enemies surround us and plot against us, Lord, rescue us from their clutches and defend us from harm. Be our strength and our salvation. Amen.

---

1. Leonard Foley and Pat McCloskey. *Saint of the Day: Lives, Lessons, and Feasts* (Cincinnati: St. Anthony Messenger Press, 2003), p. 282.

• • • | • • •
Fifth Sunday of Lent
Jeremiah: A New Covenant

YEAR A: EZEKIEL 37:12–14; PSALM 130:1–2, 3–4, 5–6, 7–8; ROMANS
8:8–11; JOHN 11:1–45

YEAR B: JEREMIAH 31:31–34; PSALM 51: 3–4, 12–13, 14–15; HEBREWS
5:7–9; JOHN 12:20–33

YEAR C: ISAIAH 43:16–21; PSALM 126:1–2A, 2B–3, 4–5, 6; PHILIPPIANS
3:8–14; JOHN 8:1–11

The figure of the prophet Jeremiah walks into our liturgy in the fifth week of Lent (on Sunday in Year B and on Friday), and his personal passion and death foreshadows that of Jesus.

In the decades before the Babylonians destroyed Jerusalem and carried its ruling class into exile, Jeremiah fearlessly confronted idolatry and the bad political alliances of Judah's kings. He paid the ultimate price after the fall of Jerusalem. Jeremiah himself was exiled to Egypt and there, tradition tells us, was murdered by some of his own people who conspired against him.

Most poignant of all his oracles is found in Jeremiah 31. There the Lord promises a "new covenant" to the people. Once again, Jeremiah anticipates Jesus. This new relationship with God will not be written on stone but on the people's hearts. They will live it so powerfully that no instruction will be necessary. "'Know the LORD,' for they shall all know me, from the least of them to the greatest, says the LORD; for I will forgive their iniquity, and remember their sin no more'" (34b).

Those to be baptized at Easter are in the final stages of their preparation. Their understanding of the relationship growing within them has passed beyond written teaching. Their friendship with the Lord has been nurtured by the community, by their sponsors, and by what God has placed in their hearts.

May we support one another in these final days of Lent and search our own hearts for what God has written there.

Today's Action
Find time to talk with those preparing for baptism in your parish and assure them of your prayers.

Prayer
Help us know you, Lord, from what you have written in our hearts. May we turn away from sin and embrace your covenant. Amen.

Monday of the Fifth Week of Lent

Margaret of Cortona: Three Stories of Mercy

DANIEL 13:1–9, 15–17, 19–30, 33–62; PSALM 23:1–3A, 3B–4, 5, 6;
JOHN 8:1–11

Two women accused of adultery are the focus of today's Scriptures. We add to the mix a lay Franciscan whose conversion from a state of public sin inspired others to penance in the thirteenth century.

From the book of Daniel comes the story of Susanna, a woman wrongly accused of adultery. It becomes the occasion for the hero of the book, young Daniel, to trap the elders who lusted after Susanna and brought the false accusation.

In the Gospel, Jesus is presented with a woman caught in adultery. Her guilt is not in question, though, under Jewish law, her partner in the sin is not on trial. Jesus challenges those publicly shaming the woman to participate in the law's required punishment of stoning —if they themselves are sinless.

No one steps forward to cast a stone, and Jesus forgives her. It's a story of mercy, and the anonymous sinner (not Mary Magdalene, as some have suggested) is freed by Jesus to turn her life around.

Margaret of Cortona was a thirteenth-century Italian orphaned at seven. She later lived with a man to whom she bore a son out of wedlock. After her partner's brutal murder, Margaret was moved to begin a life of penance. She moved with her son to Cortona. He became part of the new Franciscan movement, and Margaret eventually joined Francis' gospel life for lay persons, sometimes called the "Third Order." Known for vigorous self-denial, Margaret nursed the sick, inspired others to conversion, and founded a congregation of sisters.

Three women, three different stories. In each, God was at work. The presence of evil and the power of mercy are lessons all of us can learn on our lenten path to conversion.

Today's Action
Consider how you can support women who are victimized in today's society.

Prayer
God all-merciful, defend those falsely accused, forgive those who come to you in repentance, and strengthen us to avoid sin. Amen.

· · · | · · ·

Tuesday of the Fifth Week of Lent

Leonard of Port Maurice: Promoter of the Way of the Cross

NUMBERS 21:4–9; PSALM 102:2–3, 16–18, 19–21; JOHN 8:21–30

Today's First Reading, with the sign of the bronze serpent lifted up to cure snakebitten Israelites in the desert, parallels Jesus' statement in the Gospel that when he is "lifted up" on the cross all will recognize him and his mission from the Father. These passages put me in mind of the popular lenten devotion of the Way of the Cross.

In recent years the Holy Father has led the Way of the Cross during Holy Week at the Coliseum in Rome. This annual custom would have pleased the great Franciscan preacher Leonard of Port Maurice. In the eighteenth century he set up Stations of the Cross in 572 locations in various parts of Italy, including the Coliseum.

Leonard was a popular missionary. These preachers would travel from place to place, preaching parish missions of a week or more, giving stirring sermons and hearing confessions. Leonard was one of the greatest.

Frustrated by illness in his dream to be a foreign missionary, he took up preaching throughout Italy and spent forty years in that ministry.

Leonard mortified himself with severe penitential practices and prayer in solitude. His work bore great fruit—many conversions happened in the wake of his missions. He was also a writer and promoted the dogma of the Immaculate Conception before it was officially declared.

The Way of the Cross had long been a Catholic practice, beginning in the days when the faithful who could not go in person to the holy places associated with Jesus' death could commemorate his walk to Calvary in their local churches. But it took a zealous promoter like Leonard to popularize the practice.

Today's Action
Make the Way of the Cross at your parish church sometime this week.

Prayer
Jesus, lifted up on the cross, draw us to yourself. As we sign ourselves with your cross, remind us that we belong to you. Amen.

Wednesday of the Fifth Week of Lent

Maximilian Mary Kolbe: Witness in the Face of Cruelty

DANIEL 3:14–20, 91–92, 95; DANIEL 3:52, 53, 54, 55, 56; JOHN 8:31–42

The story of the men in the fiery furnace, from the book of Daniel, is a colorful story and the subject of a great old Gospel song. It tells the triumph of God's power in the face of a cruel king's persecution of Jewish exiles. In the twentieth century, furnaces of a different kind consumed millions of bodies in the Nazi holocaust.

Conventual Franciscan Maximilian Kolbe, imprisoned in Auschwitz in 1941, witnessed many fellow prisoners taken to the gas chambers or killed in other brutal ways. He had been interred along with Jews and others from his native Poland after Germany and the Soviet Union overran his country.

Fr. Kolbe was a high-profile religious figure, a threat to the Nazi regime. Years before, he had founded the "City of the Immaculata"—Niepokalanów, a center to promote devotion to Our Lady. Seven hundred Conventual friars lived there; a foundation also was established in Nagasaki, Japan. A million subscribers joined the "Militia of the Immaculate" and subscribed to *Knight of the Immaculate,* its religious magazine. The powerful work of prayer and witness of this group, spearhead by Fr. Kolbe, was a threat to the forces of evil unleashed in the world.

Despite the overwhelming cruelty and immense tragedy of the concentration camps, God's power was at work there. When a fellow prisoner, a family man, was singled out for execution in retaliation for a prisoner escape, Fr. Maximilian stepped forward to take his place. Starvation and lethal injection ended his earthly life but led him to the crown of martyrdom, a climax to a life of faith and devotion to the Blessed Mother and her Son.

Today's Action
Pray today for contemporary victims of genocide and persecution.

Prayer
God of Abraham, hear the cries of those who are oppressed and persecuted in our world today. Free them to lift their voices in praise of your name. Amen.

• • • | • • •

Thursday of the Fifth Week of Lent

Bernardine of Siena: Devotion to the Holy Name

GENESIS 17:3–9; PSALM 105:4–5, 6–7, 8–9; JOHN 8:51–59

When I was a boy, it was customary for Catholic men and boys from around my city to march in a "Holy Name" parade. We came from all over town and ended up at the ballpark, where an altar was set up for prayer and Benediction, the blessing with the Blessed Sacrament. This popular devotion was to counteract the improper use of the name of Jesus and to witness to the Catholic faith in a secular world. It is a devotion made popular in the fifteenth century by the Franciscan Bernardine of Siena.

Bernardine was acknowledged as a great preacher of the era. He had entered the Franciscans at age twenty-two, after spending time nursing plague victims in his hometown of Siena, Italy. After twelve years spent in prayer as a hermit, he embarked on a preaching career. He traveled throughout Italy, preaching in towns and cities.

To promote devotion to the Holy Name of Jesus, Bernardine developed a logo of sorts—the first three letters of Jesus' name, transposed into Gothic letters: *IHS*. We still see this symbol today in church art everywhere. While some thought this symbol bordered on idolatry, church authorities upheld Bernardine's innovation.

In today's Gospel, Jesus confronts his opponents in debate by appropriating to himself the divine name, I AM. His hearers interpret this as blasphemy, but Jesus is declaring the reality of who he is.

Our lenten journey must somehow come to grips with who Jesus is for us.

Bernardine of Siena creatively invited his audience to acknowledge Jesus. May we accept that invitation and also help to share it with those becoming Catholic this season.

Today's Action
Meditate for a while on the name of Jesus.

Prayer
Jesus, may your Holy Name be on our lips each day. May we accept the saving power that comes through faith in you. Amen.

Friday of the Fifth Week of Lent
Stephen: Witness to Christ
JEREMIAH 20:10–13; PSALM 18:2–3A, 3BC–4, 5–6, 7; JOHN 10:31–42

In the Gospel of John, Jesus escapes stoning by the crowds, who believe him guilty of blasphemy. That fate did not escape Stephen, the first to be martyred for believing in Jesus. The Acts of the Apostles tells Stephen's story in chapter seven, and the church celebrates his feast immediately after Christmas. But Stephen seems more a lenten saint, as he anticipates the death of Jesus.

In keeping with the debate portrayed for us in John's Gospel, as we've been hearing over these past weeks at Mass, the climactic moment comes today in John 10. The "Jews" (again, recall the caution in using this term lest we fuel an anti-Semitic attitude) pick up rocks to stone Jesus, after he claims identification with God, in the passage we read yesterday (John 8:51–59). The charge of blasphemy would be accurate if the words had been on anyone else's lips. It is a case of irony in John's Gospel that we know who Jesus truly is.

After an intense debate with certain Jews and a trial before the Sanhedrin, Stephen was condemned to be stoned for his witness to the Risen Lord. In his life and death, Stephen claims identification with Jesus and his power and presence in the world.

As we make ready for Holy Week, let's include the first martyr, Stephen, as yet another guide into the retelling of the passion, death, and resurrection of Jesus.

Today's Action
Read the story of Stephen in Acts 6 and 7.

Prayer
Jesus, may we put faith in you and in the works you do in fulfillment of the Father's will. May we help others come to believe in you. Amen.

Saturday of the Fifth Week of Lent

Catherine of Siena: A Reformer and Reconciler

EZEKIEL 37:21–28; JEREMIAH 31:10, 11–12ABCD, 13; JOHN 11:45–57

The prophet Ezekiel proclaims that the Lord will bring the Israelites back from exile and return them to their own land. Catherine of Siena may have meditated on that prophetic word, from our First Reading, as she struggled to reform the church in the fourteenth century.

Catherine was a Third Order Dominican known for her prayer, her severe ascetical practices, and her learning. Out of her periods of contemplation, she reached out in spiritual letters to enlighten and instruct others. Such activity for a woman drew suspicion and slander; Catherine was investigated and cleared of any charges of heresy.

Soon her fame spread and drew papal notice. She became a reformer and worked for unity between the papacy and civil powers. With the pope in exile, living at Avignon, France, Catherine labored to return the papacy to Rome and accomplished that goal in 1377. Her struggle for unity was severely tested during the

Great Schism beginning in 1378, when contenders for
the papacy each claimed Peter's chair (eventually there
were three papal claimants).

Today's Gospel lays out the plotting against Jesus that
will lead to his passion and death. The text reveals the
political concerns that occupy the high priests.
Catherine understood well the realities of the world but
used her spirituality, intelligence, and skills as a writer
and reconciler to assist the church in her time.

Today's Action
Use today's news headlines as a springboard for medita-
tion.

Prayer
God, who brings back the exiles, call us to our true
home in the midst of your church, where we can celebrate your love. Amen.

Palm Sunday of the Lord's Passion

Clare: Walking Into the Gospel's Challenge

PROCESSION GOSPEL:
YEAR A: MATTHEW 21:1–11; YEAR B: MARK 11:1–10 OR JOHN 12:12–16;
YEAR C: LUKE 19:28–40
FIRST READING, PSALM, SECOND READING: YEAR A, B, C:
ISAIAH 50:4–7; PSALM 22:8–9, 17–18, 19–20, 23–24; PHILIPPIANS 2:6–11
GOSPEL:
YEAR A: MATTHEW 26:14—27:66; YEAR B: MARK 14:1—15:47;
YEAR C: LUKE 22:14—23:56

To this day, pilgrims trace the steps of St. Clare on the evening of Palm Sunday 1212. She left her home, in an upper level of the city of Assisi, Italy, next to the cathedral, and made her way down, down, down, through the narrow streets, coming at last to the city gate. There, her choice to follow the gospel, in poverty and surrender to God, was made definitive as she stepped out into the night. Joined by Francis and his companions, Clare made her way to the chapel of St. Mary of the Angels, known as the Porziuncola. Her hair was cut off, symbolic of her dedication to God, and she received the simple dress of a nun.

In a film that I made in the 1990s about walking in the footsteps of Francis and Clare, we recreated Clare's walk through the night on the streets of Assisi. We could see the challenge Clare faced going into a darkened world, full of dangers.

Clare's vocation, nurtured in her family's home with her mother and sisters, had grown into a longing to live the gospel life in simple service. She identified with Francis' gospel vision, and together they forged a spiritual partnership that blossomed into a great religious family.

On this Palm Sunday, as we walk with Jesus into Jerusalem, fully aware of what awaits, let us walk with the wonder and the questions of St. Clare.

Today's Action
Make a pilgrimage of your own today, walking the streets of your neighborhood.

Prayer
Jesus, help us enter with you into the mystery of your dying and rising. May we reflect on the saving events of Holy Week and so come to Easter joy. Amen.

Monday of Holy Week

Martha and Mary: Sisters of Lazarus and Intimate Friends of Jesus

ISAIAH 42:1–7; PSALM 27:1, 2, 3, 13–14; JOHN 12:1–11

During Holy Week, the liturgy begins telling the story of the passion of Jesus. The four Gospels do not offer consistent versions of Jesus' passion and death. They know nothing of the style of reporting found in the twenty-four–hour news cycle of today! Instead, the Gospels offer theological reflection, taking common details from the tradition and shaping them to each story's purpose.

John's Gospel suggests that one event triggering the arrest of Jesus is the raising of Lazarus. In that story, we meet Martha and Mary, sisters of Lazarus, and hear them dialogue with Jesus about resurrection and life.

Today's story is a peaceful interlude in the home of these same close friends. Mary anoints Jesus' feet with expensive perfume and dries his feet with her hair. This extravagance—a very loving gesture from a friend—sparks a debate between Jesus and Judas on helping the poor.

Who among us hasn't had such an experience with friends, including heated discussions about serious topics? But John has a theological purpose: The climax of the Gospel is coming. Following this passage, Jesus enters Jerusalem and proclaims that his "hour" for him to be glorified has come. Then, echoing the scene in the Garden of Gethsemane in the other Gospels, Jesus prays to the Father, not for deliverance but for the Father to glorify his name. Jesus receives a response: The Father will do so, in all that will befall Jesus.

John is preparing us for the passion and death of Jesus. There, our Lord is in charge throughout, completing his mission as the Word made Flesh, to reveal the Father and draw those who believe into that life-giving relationship.

Today's Action
What action can you perform for Jesus to symbolize the personal dimension of your relationship with him?

Prayer
Jesus, draw us into your friendship. May we enjoy the intimacy you offer us and the life you promise. Amen.

· · · | · · ·

Tuesday of Holy Week
Peter: Waiting for the Cockcrow
Isaiah 49:1–6; Psalm 71:1–2, 3–4a, 5–6ab, 15, 17;
John 13:21–33, 36–38

Peter is a central character in the Passion narratives. On Palm Sunday each year, we hear the story of his denial of Jesus.

In John's Gospel, read today and on Holy Thursday and Good Friday, Peter is also prominent. We know what will come on Good Friday, as Peter stands in the courtyard of the high priest and blatantly denies knowing Jesus. But in today's selection, from the Last Supper, that denial is juxtaposed with the betrayal of Judas. The power of evil is at work, reaching even into the circle of Jesus' disciples. Judas leaves the supper and goes out into the night, to gather the forces to arrest Jesus.

Meanwhile, Peter is confronted with Jesus' declaration that he is leaving, going somewhere his disciples cannot follow. His question is honest: He wants to know where Jesus is going. Jesus' hour has come, and he must face it alone. In a scene reminiscent of Peter's profession of faith as depicted in the other Gospels, where he immediately rejects the way of the cross Jesus must walk, the Lord assures Peter that he cannot follow now but will later. When Peter protests that he will lay down his life for Jesus, the Lord confronts him with his impending denial.

We can be quick to distance ourselves from Peter's cowardice. But we must truthfully look at our own response as we walk these days of Holy Week. What would we do, what have we done, when called on to witness to Christ?

Today's Action
How are Peter's enthusiasm, honesty, and weakness apparent in your life?

Prayer
Jesus, help us to follow you as you walk the way of the cross. May we not lose heart in the face of suffering. Amen.

Wednesday of Holy Week

The Suffering Servant: "Here Is My Servant"

ISAIAH 50:4–9A; PSALM 69:8–10, 21–22, 31, 33–34; MATTHEW 26:14–25

Beginning on Palm Sunday, continuing Monday through Wednesday of Holy Week, and ending on Good Friday, the Liturgy of the Word presents to us a series of four special oracles. The poetic utterances by the unknown prophet whose writings are found in the second half of the book of Isaiah are often referred to as the "Songs of the Suffering Servant."

The identity of the Servant is unknown. The author may have had a contemporary figure in mind, but the context of the oracles has led contemporary scholars generally to see them as describing the "ideal Israel." This ideal represents the people who have come through the suffering of their time in exile in Babylon. They have learned from their sufferings and have let go of trying to control their own destiny. They are ready to do God's will. This transformation is described in the actions of the Servant, who has received a mission from God and carries it out in the face of opposition, physical suffering, and death.

The Suffering Servant songs are poetic and descriptive, especially the longest passage, used on Good Friday. They are worth reading and meditating on during Holy Week, since Christians have long used these Hebrew Scriptures to refer to Jesus.

The redemptive suffering of Christ is meant to teach us, transform us, and recreate us. He is our liberation, our healing, our new covenant. In the rich poetry of Isaiah, we see and hear the story of our salvation.

Today's Action
Read some of the Suffering Servant songs from Isaiah 42, 49, 50, and 52.

Prayer
Jesus, keep us faithful to you. When our faith is tested, may we not betray your trust. May we always be your servants, even in times of suffering. Amen.

Easter Triduum: Holy Thursday

Bl. John Paul II: The Witness of a Pope

EXODUS 12:1–8, 11–14; PSALM 116:12–13, 15–16, 17–18; 1 CORINTHIANS
11:23–26; JOHN 13:1–5

On Holy Thursday, 2003, Pope John Paul II issued his
final encyclical, *Ecclesia de Eucharistia*, "On the
Eucharist and Its Relationship to the Church." At the
beginning of chapter one, the pope quoted tonight's
Second Reading, from St. Paul, on the institution of the
Eucharist. The Holy Father wrote:

> The words of the Apostle Paul bring us back to the
> dramatic setting in which the Eucharist was born.
> The Eucharist is indelibly marked by the event of
> the Lord's passion and death, of which it is not only
> a reminder but the sacramental re-presentation. It
> is the sacrifice of the Cross perpetuated down the
> age.

The pope goes on to reflect on the Eucharist in the
light of the events celebrated in these days, as Lent ends
and we enter the Easter Triduum (the great "three
days"). While the chronology of the three days follows

the Passion narrative, the liturgy is not "playacting" the events marking Jesus' passage from death to life. Rather, we are invited into that mystery through the Scriptures and the liturgical celebrations, especially the initiation of new Christians in the sacraments of baptism, confirmation, and Eucharist at the Easter Vigil.

Bl. Pope John Paul II in his life, his ministry as pope, and especially his dying, lived that mystery. In his final days he taught us how to join our human suffering to the sufferings of Christ. In so doing, the Holy Father gave us his last witness to the truths he so eloquently described in his encyclical on the Eucharist.

Today's Action
Take time to read some of *Ecclesia de Eucharistia*, available in English translation at www.vatican.va.

Prayer
Jesus, feed us with your Body and Blood, and strengthen us to be your body in the world, ready to serve others as you served your disciples at the Last Supper. Amen.

· · · | · · ·
Easter Triduum: *Good Friday*
Mary: A Mother at the Foot of the Cross
Isaiah 52:13—53:12; Psalm 31:2, 6, 12–13, 15–16, 17, 25; Hebrews
4:14–16; 5:7–9; John 18:1—19:42

"No mother should bear the death of her son." I heard that sentiment expressed in my family as a teenager, when my favorite uncle died of cancer in his forties. My grandmother was never the same afterward. The Stations of the Cross capture similar feelings, at the fourteenth station, popularly known as the Pietà. It is a scene full of grief, a mother holding the lifeless body of her son.

John's Passion story, read on Good Friday, depicts Mary at the foot of the cross. Standing next to the disciple whom Jesus loved, Mary hears Jesus say, "Woman, here is your son." And to the Beloved Disciple he says, "Here is your mother" (John 19:26–27). In human terms, this is a tender moment of a dying son entrusting his mother to a friend's care. But the fourth Gospel emphasizes Jesus' triumph on the cross, a moment of glory. It is not a tragic scene of suffering mother and son.

With this exchange, Mary is symbolically transformed. Where once she gave physical life to Jesus at his birth, she now symbolizes the church, which gives us the life of Jesus.

When the soldier pierces Jesus' side with the spear, blood and water flow out. The church, present at the cross, receives the life of the sacraments from Jesus, just as he has "handed over his spirit."

Mary fulfills her role as the "Virgin made Church," as she is called in one of the prayers of St. Francis of Assisi. As she gave birth to the Savior, she is now present at the birth of the church from the cross.

Today's Action
Pray the sorrowful mysteries of the rosary today.

Prayer
Jesus, we stand with Mary at the foot of your cross. Entrust us to her care. May she ever lead us to you in the heart of the church. Amen.

・ ・ ・ | ・ ・ ・

Easter Triduum: Holy Saturday / Easter Vigil

Mary Magdalene: Witness to Death and Resurrection

*The Vigil offers a choice of eight readings from
the Old Testament, with psalm responses.*

EXODUS 14:15—15:1 MUST ALWAYS BE USED. ROMANS 6:3–11;
PSALM 118:1–2, 16–17, 22–23;
GOSPEL:
YEAR A: MATTHEW 28:1–10; YEAR B: MARK 16:1–7;
YEAR C: LUKE 24:1–12

Mary Magdalene is one of the main characters in the story of Jesus' passion, death, and resurrection.

Mary was not a public sinner. Nor was she the figure who anointed Jesus' feet with her tears or wiped them with her hair. She was, however, a faithful disciple. Unlike the male disciples, who fled from Jesus' crucifixion, Mary was present. Matthew and Mark place her among those "looking on from a distance" (Matthew 27:55–56; Mark 15:40). Luke identifies her, as do the other Gospels, with the women who went to the tomb to anoint the body of Jesus.

We can imagine what she must have endured after Jesus' violent death. Like anyone who had put hope in Jesus, Mary must have been devastated. In John 20, we witness her great grief and her anxiety as she discovers the empty tomb. John then helps us imagine her joy and wonder when Jesus, the Good Shepherd, meets her in the garden, calls her by name, and gives her a mission to announce his resurrection to the other disciples.

Mary Magdalene becomes the first to witness to the Risen Lord. We have spent Lent in prayer and penance to prepare us to renew our baptismal identity. Tonight we welcome those becoming Christian and entering into full communion with the church. May Mary Magdalene inspire the newly baptized and received, and all of us, to take our Easter joy into the world!

Today's Action
Read the stories of Mary Magdalene in the Gospels and reflect on her true role in Jesus' passion, death, and resurrection.

Prayer
Jesus, help us imitate Mary Magdalene as your faithful disciple. May we seek you, hear your voice calling us, and be your witnesses in the world. Amen.

· · · | · · ·

Easter Triduum: *Easter Sunday*

The Beloved Disciple: It's All About Love

Acts 10:34a, 37–43; Psalm 118:1–2, 16–17, 22–23; Colossians 3:1–4
or 1 Corinthians 5:6b–8; John 20:1–9

In 1984 singer Tina Turner had a comeback hit with her recording of "What's Love Got to Do With It." Years later I drew a lot of smiles when I began an Easter Sunday homily with the song's title. It's a question that explains the Easter Gospel, John 20:1–9, which tells us that Peter and the "disciple Jesus loved" came to the tomb early on the first day of the week after hearing Mary Magdalene's report of the empty tomb.

The Beloved Disciple arrives first but waits until Peter enters and sees Jesus' burial wrappings neatly folded. Peter doesn't understand what he sees. But the other disciple is moved to an act of faith. He's the disciple whom Jesus loved, and love leads to faith. That's what love has to do with it!

The characters in John's Easter story show various stages of belief. Mary Magdalene believes when she is prompted by the Lord himself, when they meet in the garden near the tomb. Peter gets to wipe out his denials of Jesus with three affirmation of love when he encounters Jesus on the seashore (John 21). Doubting Thomas, a fourth character in John's resurrection story, needs visible proof before he will believe (John 20).

I can find myself in all of these gospel portraits by John. Sometimes I want proof, like Thomas, or I need forgiveness, like Peter. I pray that my faith can be that of the Beloved Disciple, who understood what love has to do with it.

Today's Action
Look back on your Lent. How has your faith grown during this time?

Prayer
Risen Lord, thank you for sharing your life with us. May love move us to faith, as we renew the promises of our baptism today. Amen.

• • • | • • •

Saints and Feast Days

Alphonsus Liguori (August 1)

André Bessette (January 6)

Anthony of Padua (June 13)

Augustine (August 28)

Bernardine of Siena (May 20)

Catherine of Siena (April 29)

Clare (August 11)

Cornelius and Cyprian (September 16)

Damien Joseph de Veuster of Molokai (May 10)

Frances of Rome (March 9)

Francis de Sales (January 24)

Gianna Beretta Molla (April 28)

Ignatius of Loyola (July 31)

Isidore the Farmer (May 15)

James (July 25)

Bl. John Paul II (October 22)

John (December 27)

John Vianney (August 4)

Leonard of Port Maurice (November 26)

Margaret of Cortona (May 16)

Martha and Mary (July 29)

Martin de Porres (November 3)

Mary Magdalene (July 22)

Matthew (Levi) (September 21)

Maximilian Mary Kolbe (August 14)

Patrick (March 17)

Paul (June 29)

Pio of Pietrelcina (Padre Pio) (September 23)

Sharbel Makhluf (July 24)

Stephen (December 26)

Teresa of Avila (October 15)

Bl. Teresa of Calcutta (September 5)

Thérèse of the Child Jesus (October 1)

Thomas More (June 22)

About the Author

Greg Friedman, O.F.M., is a media producer and author of *Advent With the Saints: Daily Reflections*. He is host of *American Catholic Radio*, a program syndicated on Catholic radio stations nationwide. In 2009 his film *Assisi Pilgrimage: Walking in Faith With Francis and Clare* appeared on PBS. Fr. Greg is also pastor of an inner-city parish in Cincinnati, Ohio.

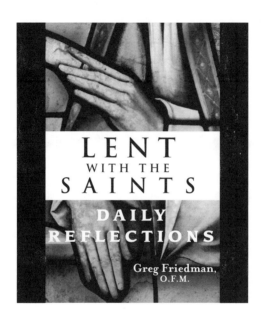

LENT
WITH THE
SAINTS

DAILY
REFLECTIONS

Greg Friedman,
O.F.M.

ST. ANTHONY MESSENGER PRESS
Cincinnati, Ohio

RESCRIPT

In accord with the *Code of Canon Law,* I hereby grant my permission to publish *Lent With the Saints: Daily Reflections* by Greg Friedman, O.F.M.

Most Reverend Joseph R. Binzer
Auxiliary Bishop
Vicar General
Archdiocese of Cincinnati
Cincinnati, Ohio
September 2, 2011

Cover and book design by Mark Sullivan
Cover image © Veer